I0559295

SAINT
ANTHONY

THE SAINT OF THE WHOLE WORLD

REV. THOMAS F. WARD

SENSUS FIDELIUM PRESS

Gastonia, North Carolina

For more information, please visit sensusfideliumpress.com

St. Anthony is not only the Saint of Padua, he is the Saint of the whole world.

—Leo XIII

Nihil Obstat.

Remy Lafort, *Censor Librorum.*

Imprimatur

* Michael Augustine, *Archbishop of New York.*

PREFACE

If ever man, if ever saint received the Holy Spirit abundantly, it was unquestionably the saint whose life we now present for the edification of the faithful. I It was by the Holy Spirit and His sevenfold gifts that St. Anthony accomplished those great wonders which we admire in his life. Supernatural light and piety and strength were the means which God furnished him, and by which he so marvelously fulfilled his mission.

When the Savior wished to save men, He commenced His ministry by instructing them. He preached in Judea and in Galilee, in fact He declared that His mission was precisely to preach to men. When He was about to ascend to heaven, He charged His apostles to continue the work He had begun and insisted that they also should preach His word to men.

Yet let us not suppose that preaching consists merely in the discourses which the apostle delivered: "No," said a great preacher, "the apostle is not only a man who knows, and who teaches by means of the word delivered; the apostle is a man who preaches Christianity with his whole being, and whose very presence is the appearance of another Christ."

And such was St. Anthony of Padua, to whom devotion is so widespread to-day. This amiable saint was at once both monk and apostle. To the preaching of the Gospel, he added the strict observance of the severest counsels and the constant practice of fasting, of penance, and of prayer. It was by these means that he captivated countless followers: the just were strengthened, the slothful fired with zeal, sinners were converted, and heretics recognized their errors. At the comparatively early age of thirty-six years his earthly mission ended. After his death, even as during his life, wonders were wrought through his intercession. And now, after seven centuries have passed away, the great wonderworker still spreads out his blessings on those who invoke him, with such profusion as is well calculated to encourage his devout servants to continue the offering of their homage.

It is for this end that we devote these few pages, which will proclaim the virtues of this great friend of God, and the power he possesses in heaven.

To render to the saints the honor, which is due them, we should invoke and imitate them. We should strive to follow the good examples which they have given us while on earth; and to do this we should read and know their lives.

Let us read especially the life of St. Anthony of Padua, and we shall be astonished at such exalted sanctity. We cannot fail to admire the power granted by God to this wonderworker.

Devotion to St. Anthony of Padua crossed the ocean with our fathers, and with the Virgin Mother and St. Joseph he is invoked in almost every Catholic household, with a fervor and a piety which, we must admit, have received their fullest recompense.

Who can deny the power of St. Anthony, especially in certain circumstances? When we read this little book, we shall learn, after the example the saint has given us, that there is everything to gain by serving God faithfully and lovingly, while there is everything to lose by abandoning Him.

We shall learn also the great advantages which follow the invocation of the saints, and how much our sorrows shall be soothed, if we only know how to form friendships in heaven.

CONTENTS

1. INFANCY OF ST. ANTHONY OF PADUA   1

2. HIS VOCATION   4

3. ST. ANTHONY ENTERS THE HOUSE OF THE FRIARS MINOR   7

4. ST. ANTHONY LECTURES ON THEOLOGY   10

5. ST. ANTHONY AND THE ALBIGENSES   15

6. ST. ANTHONY IS APPOINTED CUSTODIAN OF LIMOGES.   21

7. THE WONDER-WORKER AT LIMOGES   24

8. ST. ANTHONY LEAVES FRANCE   31

9. ST. ANTHONY IN ITALY—THE MIRACLE OF THE FISHES   35

10. ST. ANTHONY AT PADUA   41

11. GENERAL CHAPTER OF ASSISI   45

12. DEATH OF ST. ANTHONY   49

13. THE BREAD OF ST. ANTHONY   57

14. WHAT IS ASKED OF ST. ANTHONY   63

15. PRAYERS TO ST. ANTHONY   66

INFANCY OF ST. ANTHONY OF PADUA

St. Anthony of Padua was born at Lisbon, in Portugal, on the 15th day of August 1195. His father was Martin de Bouillon and his mother Theresa de Tavera. Both were descended from a long line of ancient and illustrious ancestors, remarkable for their courage and faith and their nobility of blood.

Hardly had the illustrious St. Francis of Assisi been called to his reward, then his place was filled, in the veneration and enthusiasm of the people, by him whom all proclaimed his firstborn, the amiable saint of whom we are speaking. Like his spiritual father, St. Anthony was remarkable for his dominion over nature which won for him the title of wonderworker.

The newly born child was carried in great pomp to the sacred precincts of the cathedral, and there received the name of Fernando.

There was unbounded joy in the household: the lowly and the great ones united their congratulations, and the palace of the de Bouillon resounded with best wishes, which might seem exaggerated, to be excelled only by the reality. His mother, Donna Theresa, was most conscientious in her duties, and realized her responsibility fully. Her solicitude was very great in the exercise of her exalted mission, which for every mother worthy of the name is a sacred obligation. Being thoroughly Christian, she filled the mind of her little son with the sweet teachings of the Gospel, and being the daughter of heroes, she formed him on lofty ideals of character, and to esteem those great things which she regarded as the most beautiful possession of nobility.

This pious mother, full of devotion to the Queen of Heaven, taught her beloved child not only Mary's power and goodness, but she taught him also to give her his confidence and love.

Fernando responded to the affection of his mother. Everything in him foretold a heart of gold and an exalted and refined intelligence. He was happy only when they spoke to him of the Blessed Trinity, the Virgin Mother, and the saints. The ardor with which he recited his daily devotions was the admiration of everyone. We might say that his education was given him in the church, at the foot of the altars, and that his science was founded especially oil the knowledge of religion. He learned the Latin language rapidly, and, in fact, all that was taught in the schools at the time: humanities, rhetoric, and philosophy. Everything that related to religion, ecclesiastical history, and to liturgy was for him an object of marked predilection. His devotion to study, his modesty, his sweetness, and his piety were the consolation of his preceptors and the, admiration of his comrades. He was regarded as the model of all the virtues, and merited even more eulogies than were bestowed upon him.

The first miracle of which we have any record took place in the church which he was accustomed to frequent. One day, as he was kneeling on the steps of the altar, in the sanctuary of Our Lady of the Pillar and his eyes fixed on the tabernacle, this angel of the earth mingled his burning adorations with those of his brethren in heaven. Suddenly the demon appeared to him in a threatening manner, striving to turn him away from his devotions. The terrified young man remembered the power of the sign of the cross, and quickly he traced this sign on the marble steps. At once, under the impress of his pure and delicate finger, the marble softened and retained the impression of the cross. It was a thunder-stroke for the demon, who immediately disappeared. The miraculous cross is visible to this day, and pilgrims love to kiss the ineffaceable mark of the first prodigy in a life all resplendent with prodigies.

HIS VOCATION

In time the young Fernando attained to manhood, the age when the
passions grow strong, the moment of deceitful dreams and delusions,
the critical epoch of life, the dangerous shoal on which so many
beautiful souls are shipwrecked and forever ruined. Fernando was
surrounded by countless snares. Being rich, and of illustrious birth
and splendid personal appearance, he was exposed to all the attacks of
the world, and besides he lived in a city which then, as now, was truly a
place of pleasure. But he did not yield to temptation: chosen souls, like
this one, are even more exposed than others to dangers, temptations,
and ruin. While, it is true, he was strong to combat against himself
and against the demon, his heart, however, was swayed by great trials;
but God was with him and He never abandoned His servant. In those
moments when he felt himself failing, he had recourse to God and
the Virgin Mother, his patroness, and with tearful eyes asked their
protection and assistance. One day, raised by grace above the world
and himself, he resolved to delay no longer in consecrating himself to
God. "O world!" he cried, "thou hast overwhelmed me; thy strengthen
only a frail reed, thy riches are only a little smoke andthy pleasures so

many quicksands in which one is shipwrecked. For me, O Lord, Thy alone shall be my dwelling forever." His resolution was taken, firm and irrevocable. He asked for the habit in the convent of Canons Regular of St. Augustine, at Lisbon. He was received with open arms and the white robe of the novices placed upon him.

Fernando was happy; now he had only to think of God. But he was not allowed long to enjoy that peace which he desired with so much ardor. His parents and friends, during the year of his novitiate, tormented him constantly to return to the world. Every means were employed; caresses, threats, flatteries, and bitter railleries. Being harassed on every side, fatigued by constant combat which detached his soul from the pure joys of the sanctuary, the young novice resolved to depart from Lisbon, and to seek elsewhere the tranquility he could not find there. He decided to go to Coimbra, where, as at Lisbon, he was the admiration of the other religious.

In the abbey, the study of letters and the vision of the religious life went hand-in-hand, and so Don Fernando could give himself to the pursuit of sacred science. Nature richly endowed him. His memory was prodigious. He retained whatever he read. Being alone with God, meditating constantly on heave and holy things, he soon acquired a full and complete knowledge of them. It was said that the Holy Spirit had descended on him as upon the Apostles to give him the gift of tongues, immense knowledge, and an irresistible eloquence. His preceptors did not conceal their admiration for his vast erudition, and his superiors did not hesitate to present him for sacred orders.

Moreover, the sanctity of this servant of God was already known by miracles. One day, as he was occupied near the church at some humble occupation, he heard the clock strike suddenly, which announced the time of the elevation. As he knelt on the earth, he beheld the stone walls open before him, and the priest at the altar appeared to him, holding the sacred Host in his hands.

On another day, while attending a sick brother, who laughed and cried alternately, as if afflicted nervously, the idea came to Anthony that the unhappy brother was under the power of the demon—and so it was in fact: taking his mantle from his shoulders he covered the afflicted brother, who was at once restored to perfect health.

On another occasion, while assisting the priest at the altar, he perceived the soul of a Franciscan religious suspended in the air under the form of a white dove. The soul had passed through purgatory, had paid the last farthing of satisfaction, and entered into the kingdom of the elect.

ST. ANTHONY ENTERS THE HOUSE OF THE FRIARS MINOR

In the year 1216, St. Francis of Assisi had just sent into Portugal St. Zachary and St. Gauthier with some Friars Minor. King Alphonsus II. had confided to them the chapel of the holy abbe Anthony, about half a league from Coimbra, and made them erect there a convent. As they often came to collect at the houses of the Augustinians, Don Fernando soon knew them, and consequently admired the austerity of their apostolic life. He loved to converse with them and felt in his heart an immense desire to imitate them. There was also another circumstance which influenced him, viz.: the solemn translation of the bodies of five Franciscan religious who had just been martyred at Maroc. On learning the glorious history of these five apostles, he also wished to shed his blood for Christ by propagating the faith. Day and night he longed for the palm of martyrdom, which he believed he could merit only under the habit of the Friars Minor.

After praying to God to make known to him His intentions, he imparted his desire and his resolutions to the Brothers of St. Anthony des Oliviers, who received him with great joy.

Great indeed was the sorrow of the Augustinian Canons when they had learned his determination. The prior, in giving him the permission he could not refuse, did not conceal his disapprobation, and one of the Canons to whom he bade adieu said to him with sorrow: "Go, you will perhaps become a saint." But Fernando answered humbly: "The day on which you learn that I have become a saint you shall be the first to give thanks to God for it."

The new Franciscan received, with the habit of the Order, the name of Anthony in honor of the holy priest to whom was dedicated the first seraphic convent in Portugal.

When he had pronounced his vows, remembering he had entered the seraphic Order only with the desire of gaining the crown of martyrdom, he asked his superiors for permission to go to Africa to preach there the truth to the Maurians. His superiors allowed him to depart; but God, who was content with his ardent desire, had decided in His eternal wisdom that Anthony should exercise his zeal in Europe. He had scarcely reached the end of his journey when our saint fell a victim to a cruel illness which more than once placed his life in danger and forced him to return to Portugal, where he expected to find health and strength. The return was unfortunate; a violent tempest cast him on the shores of Sicily.

He then went to Messina, where the Brothers Minor had a convent; and about two months after the servant of God was fully restored to health. There was at that time an official convocation of the Fourth General Chapter of the Order, and our saint hastened to place himself at the disposition of the holy founder.

The Chapter opened at Portiuncula on the thirtieth day of May 1221. It was a most imposing assembly; the bishop, the cardinal, and about three thousand brethren assembled from the north and south. But above and beyond all, the seraphic patriarch was conspicuous not only because of the superiority of his virtues, but because of his authority. Anthony never tired contemplating the emaciated and worn countenance expressive of humility, zeal, and love; nor could he thank the divine Master sufficiently for having called him to a warfare so providentially sent to the assistance of His Church. St. Francis, so largely endowed with the discernment of souls, did not know this son, who was destined soon to shed luster on the institute. He divided the labors, assigned residences, and pointed out the new missions. But in all these arrangements Anthony was overlooked. No provincial thought of claiming him. He was looked upon as a novice, as one incapable of duty. God permitted this humiliation to strengthen the merits of His faithful servant. He reserved him for the proper time, to place him as a bright light in a most conspicuous place.

The blessed Anthony begged to be allowed to accompany the provincial so that he might be formed or trained in the exercises of the regular discipline. Not one word of his past life escaped his lips, not the least allusion to his theological studies. To know Jesus and Jesus crucified, and to love Him—such was his desire. Touched by the exquisite candor of the applicant, the provincial granted his request, embraced him tenderly, and together they set out for Roumania.

ST. ANTHONY LECTURES ON THEOLOGY

As Brother Anthony was a priest, the provincial appointed him to attend the little monastery of St. Paul on the mountain of the same name. The convent was admirably situated on the summit of the mountain, suspended, so to speak, between earth and heaven, where no earthly sound could reach it. There the ravished soul could hear in silence and peace the great harmonies of nature celebrating the grandeur and the power of the Creator.

This was precisely what Anthony always longed for; a religious gave him a little cell built in the rock, on the side of the mountain. There it was he came, when his duties were fulfilled, to pass days and nights in perpetual meditation, interrupted only by austere practices. He lived on bread and water, and wore under his clothing a hair shirt, sharp and coarse, all of which are still preserved at Padua in a silver frame. His mortifications weakened him so much that he could scarcely stand. But if the body was weak, the soul was strong, being constantly strengthened by prayer, and prepared to combat victoriously against heresy and all the vanities of the world.

Anthony lived thus for a whole year in solitude and contemplation, submissive to the providence of God, which he never questioned for a moment.

The time, however, approached when the pious Anthony should make known the precious gifts he had received from heaven. In the year 1222, the servant of God accompanied the Friars Minor who went to Forli to receive sacred orders. It was the custom, after an ordination, to address some words to the young clerics, who had just been ordained ministers of the Most High.

The bishop of Forli requested the guardian of Mount St. Paul to discharge this duty, or to entrust it to one of his religious. The eyes of the superior fell on Anthony, and it was he who received the command, in the name of holy obedience, to ascend the pulpit and give the customary discourse. Against his feelings he consented, esteeming himself unworthy of such an honor. Yet he must obey; and, having asked the bishop's blessing, he prepared himself to speak. None of his assistants thought that he had studied the Holy Scriptures or had scarcely read them; they saw him constantly engaged in the kitchen, occupied in cleansing the vessels of the convent rather than plunged in the works of high theology.

He took for his text this passage of the office for Holy Thursday, *Christus factus est obediens usque ad mortem.* At first his words were calm, without splendor, almost hesitating. Then he became animated, rapid, energetic, and burning. The poor monk, worn out by sufferings and privations, and of wretched appearance, spoke with the authority of an apostle and the eloquence of a prophet. With his powerful voice and superb gestures, he ruled the whole assembly. By his attitude alone he seemed to say, "Listen, children of men, for I am he who speaks in the name of the Lord." In fact, he was heard with religious admiration. The assistants were mute with astonishment and shed tears of happiness. They saw a ray of divine intelligence shining in him and were penetrated by a profound and holy respect. A new life had now begun for Anthony.

The public reports and the comments of his superiors were not slow in making known to the holy patriarch Francis what had been the success of the first sermon pronounced by the young religious, and also what magnificent hopes were expected from such a beginning. Almost at once he was entrusted with the difficult mission of laboring for the conversion and the salvation of souls. Anthony was then only twenty-seven years old.

From the day on which he began his painful and glorious labor until he ceased to preach, an attentive and pious multitude eagerly thronged to hear his sermons. At first, he evangelized the principal cities of Roumania and Lombardy. Success crowned his efforts beyond all hope. Sinners wept and sobbed in the churches where he preached, and the most unexpected conversions were wrought by his labors. His words were like so many darts which pierced the hearts of his hearers. He gave to others of his own fulness; and it was not astonishing that, having kindled in his own soul the fire of divine charity, he enkindled it also in the souls of all who heard him.

The superiority of Anthony's talents responded to a project cherished for three or four years by the seraphic patriarch. He wished to have an official course of theology for the special use of the Order. The venerable founder looked about him, among all his disciples, for a wise and well- balanced mind, uniting solid piety with vast wisdom. He was still seeking when the Superior Gratien presented, in eulogistic terms, the contemplative of Mount St. Paul as the type of the accomplished director. At once the patriarch of Assisi selected Anthony, and he was too obedient a son to think for an instant of declining the honor offered him, in spite of his extreme modesty. Well did he know that the honor was also a heavy charge. Immediately leaving the grotto of Mount St. Paul which he loved so well, he hastened to Bologna, there to fulfil the office of preacher. In addition to his preaching, he professed theology, at first in France, at Montpelier, then at Bologna, and at Padua, then at Toulouse, and in several other cities of France. Everywhere a multitude of young men, thirsting for science, gathered to hear his lessons; and his fame increased from day to day in spite of the efforts he made to remain unknown, although he did not think of himself but of the souls of his hearers.

The learned abbe of St. Andrew said of Anthony: "Love often passes the limits in which science dwells; and this is what I have observed in Anthony, the friar minor, with whom I have had friendly relations for a long time; he had not only a very profound knowledge of human science, but by the purity of his soul and the fire of his love he has surpassed the greatest theologians, and we can say of him, as of St. John the Baptist, he was as a lamp which burns by consuming itself. The fire of his love consumed him, and by the example of his holy life he enlightened the world." Anthony also loved this learned abbe tenderly, and as often as he passed near Piedmont, he never neglected to visit him. At the moment of his death, he suddenly appeared to the theologian, who, lost in his books, was suffering from a violent headache. Anthony affectionately embraced him and said: "I have left my work at Padua and am returning to my country." Having relieved the headache, he vanished as a phantom. The abbe, imagining that Anthony was returning to Portugal, searched the convent, and was astonished to find that no one had seen him. Some days afterward everything was explained; he received the news from Padua that

Anthony had died, and precisely at the hour when he had appeared to him.

ST. ANTHONY AND THE ALBIGENSES

At this epoch the heresy of the Albigenses began to work its ravages in the south of France. Like a contagious scourge, it spread in the cities and villages and made countless victims. St. Francis was moved by it; his heart was bleeding at the thought of the sorrows which countless souls were preparing for themselves in eternity, and he thought he could arrest the progress of the evil. For this great mission he selected Anthony and charged him to found convents of the Order, and to preach the true faith in Provence and Languedoc. Anthony departed feeling strong in the help of the Lord.

Hardly had he arrived when he gave himself resolutely to the work assigned him. He labored incessantly, without truce or intermission, until the heresy was reduced almost to powerlessness. He was called the *hammer of heresy.* Conversions were frequent. Each sermon gained a great number. When he ceased speaking many men and women approached him with tears in their eyes, to ask of him, in the name of the Lord, pardon and absolution for their errors. Moreover, he spared himself no fatigue. After his daily Mass he passed his days in preaching, in catechizing, in giving wise counsel, and in absolving. So engrossed was he in these works of charity and love he forgot to eat or drink. Oftentimes, he took his first repast only when night was coming on. At night he prayed, meditated, and studied. The Lord took care to confirm his words by prodigies.

One morning, while our saint was in the pulpit, the body of a young man was brought to him, who had been prematurely taken from his parents. The sorrow of the family was heart-rending. The blessed Anthony was profoundly moved and suspended his preaching for a few moments. Then extending his hand towards the coffin, he cried out in a tone of authority, "In the name of Christ, young man, arise!" At the sound of his voice the young man stirred, tore off his shroud, and cast himself into the arms of his parents, who, needless to say, were filled with joy and gratitude.

In 1225 he preached in the Church of Montpelier, on a festival day, in presence of the clergy and a countless multitude. At the beginning of his discourse, he remembered that he had been appointed to sing in the choir during the solemn Mass, which was celebrated at the same hour in the chapel of the convent, and he had neglected to delegate someone in his place. He was deeply afflicted at this forgetfulness and regarded his conduct as an infraction of the law of obedience. He bowed his head on the pulpit, and enveloped himself in his hood, and there remained a long time motionless and silent, to the great astonishment of all present. At the same time, he appeared in the midst of his brethren, sang the Alleluia, and fulfilled his duty. About one hour after he again stood up in the pulpit and continued with incomparable eloquence the sermon he had only commenced.

Great was the sorrow of our saint one day, when on entering his cell he perceived that his "Commentary on the Psalms" had disappeared. A novice who had wearied of religious life secretly took the book and had departed. Not knowing whom he might charge with the theft, as usual he had recourse to prayer, and conjured Him to whom nothing is hidden to recover his loss. At the same moment the fugitive was arrested in his flight. On the banks of a river, a hideous specter suddenly appeared before him, and said: "In the name of the Lord, restore what you have stolen, otherwise I shall kill you and cast you into the depths of the abyss." The terrified novice retraced his steps, made an avowal of his faults, and asked for pardon with many tears, and with such sincerity that St. Anthony restored him the religious habit with most paternal affection. The Lord granted him personal favors, and we shall see further on how he gained the permanent and universal privilege of finding things which had been lost.

St. Anthony preached at a station at Bourges, and so great was the multitude desiring to hear him that the churches of the city were unable to accommodate them. It was determined to assemble in the open air, at the foot of a small eminence. Suddenly lightning flashed and the thunder groaned, and the blackened clouds spread out over the blue vault of heaven until they had obscured and hidden everything. The people were terrified and wished to flee and seek some shelter. But Anthony tranquillized them.

"Remain in peace," he said to the assistants, "not one drop of rain shall touch you." He continued to speak as if he were in the pulpit of the cathedral. The storm raged with fury around the pious assembly but left untouched the space they occupied.

At the arrival of Anthony, the war between error and truth, appeased by the preaching of St. Dominic some years before, was again enkindled and with more bitterness than ever. His work extended everywhere, when faith was in danger. During the year 1225 this servant of God arrived at Toulouse, where he found the Albigenses in possession of all their liberties, thanks to the protection of Count Raymond VII. Besides, the heretics continued to teach their doctrines in the streets and byways, a doctrine which saddened the ears of the angels and shocked the faith of the Christians. Anthony at once with all his zeal began to lead these lost souls into the bosom of truth. Night and day he disputed with the heretics; in their presence he expounded the Catholic teaching with greatest clearness; he victoriously refuted their prejudices, employing such learning as was calculated **to** win their admiration, and a charity which found its way to their hearts and converted them.

Among the errors professed by the Albigenses was the denial of the Real Presence of Our Lord in the blessed Eucharist. One day St. Anthony carried on a long discussion on this article of Catholic faith with an obstinate and influential heretic of the city. Being pressed by the solid and luminous reasons of the apostle, the heretic seemed to waver, even to the point of giving homage to faith. He stopped short, however, even as the Jews of old, and asked for miracles. "Prove to me by a public miracle," he said, "that Jesus is really present in the Eucharist, as you are striving to establish, and I swear to you that I shall at once renounce my doctrines, and humbly submit myself to what you preach." The challenge was a solemn one; another would have hesitated to accept it. But Anthony, inspired by the Holy Spirit, tranquilly replied he would accept it. Then the heretic said: "I shall shut my mule in his stable for three days, and deprive him of all food. When this time shall have passed, I will lead him into the public street and before all the assembled people I will offer him food to eat. But you, on your part, will bring the consecrated Host and will present it to my mule. If, in spite of his hunger he turns away from the food, and prostrates himself on both knees before your sacrament, I shall be convinced, and declare myself a Catholic." Anthony consented to this proposition and departed. He prepared himself by prayer to avenge Jesus for the outrages inflicted on Him by the impiety of the Manicheans. He asked of God to draw from the slavery of error so many simple souls, over whom the torrent of opinion triumphed, and led far from His Church. At length the day of trial came, and the heretic came to the appointed place, followed by a large number who hoped to enjoy the confusion of the Franciscan apostle. The heretic led his mule by the bridle, and carried the food which he knew would be so welcome. During this time Anthony celebrated Mass with even greater fervor than ordinary. When he had finished, he turned towards the scene where the power of Heaven was soon to be manifested. The saint held in his hands the golden ostensorium, in the center of which reposed the Lamb who takes away the sins of the world. Behind him walked many of the faithful, reciting prayers and hymns, impatient to see what would happen. When Anthony was in the presence of his adversary, he stopped and recollected himself for an instant; then he imposed silence on the multitude, and turning to the mule thus spoke to him: "In the name of thy Creator, whom I truly carry in my hands, in spite of my unworthiness, I say to thee, O animal deprived of reason, and I command thee, to come at once with humility and do Him the reverence which you owe Him." At the same moment the owner of the mule presented him with food to eat. But, O prodigy! the beast turned away from his food, and, obedient to the voice of the wonderworker, fell to the earth on both knees and remained in this position immovable. The people, breathless with wonder, could not contain their enthusiasm; and cries of joy escaped from everyone. The heretics were cast on the ground where they stood, while the one who had provoked the miracle fell on his knees and adored in a loud voice the august Mystery, which a moment before he had called a superstition. He afterwards became an apostle, brought back to the truth his whole family, and constructed, at his own expense, a church which he dedicated to St. Peter. His descendants, to add to his gratitude, and to perpetuate the memory of the miracle, built a chapel on the very spot where the miracle had been wrought.

It was at Toulouse that the Blessed Virgin appeared to our saint to tell him that three days after her death she had been transported into heaven, body and soul, and that since that blessed day she was seated in glory at the right hand of Jesus, her Son. At this epoch the belief in the assumption of Mary was not so strong as today. Anthony felt his heart expand with love for the Virgin Mother, which was not a new thing for him, but strengthened by the visit of the Virgin he proclaimed her glory everywhere.

ST. ANTHONY IS APPOINTED CUSTODIAN OF LIMOGES.

A short time after Anthony left Toulouse and went to the convent of Puy-en-Velay, of which he had been appointed guardian. The city of Puy and the country roundabout soon knew the apostle, whose fame had already preceded him. Le Velay was not able to escape the invasion of heresy; but Anthony soon arrested the ravages of error. He employed all his energy to combat them, until he had destroyed and radically extirpated them. At the sound of his voice the true religion awakened in the hearts of these brave people, who hastened in crowds to listen to his preaching. His mission here was easy. From the beginning to the end there were constant miracles and prophecies, conversions and providential circumstances which rendered his missions most fruitful.

The first remarkable fact was the conversion of a notary, a man of lax morals and of violent character. Every time that Anthony met him in the streets the saint stopped and bowed profoundly before him. Irritated by what he regarded as a mockery, the notary avoided meeting his supposed insulter. One day, seeing the saint bending his knee before him, he angrily said: "What do you mean by these grimaces? Did I not fear the anger of God, I would pierce you with my sword." "My brother," Anthony replied, in a voice as calm and sweet as becomes a disciple of St. Francis, "I desire your happiness. I wish for martyrdom, but Our Lord does not so will it—yet He has revealed to me that He has reserved this grace for you. When this blessed hour shall come for you, remember, I beg of you, him who foretold it to you." The notary laughed uproariously at what he considered a senseless prediction. Some years after, however, Stephen III., bishop of Puy, set out with a troop of pilgrims to visit the holy places and to carry the torch of faith to the East. The notary, touched by grace and resolved to repair his scandals, joined the pious caravan. Having arrived at Palestine, he did not fear to assert his faith, and cry out to the Mussulmans that Mahomet was only an impostor. For this he was arrested and condemned to death. As he walked to the scaffold he remembered the prophecy of Anthony and spoke of it to the Franciscans who exhorted him to be brave in his martyrdom.

On another day, in the same city of Puy, a lady of quality, about to become a mother, recommended herself to the prayers of St. Anthony. "Rejoice," he replied, as if by sudden inspiration; "the Lord will give you a son who shall be a member of the Friars Minor, and he shall be a martyr and illustrious in the Church." The prediction was fulfilled literally.

His was a magnanimous soul, which stopped at no personal consideration, an intrepid missionary who did not hesitate to speak the truth to great and small, to prelates as well as to the simple faithful, when the honor of the Church or the good of souls required it. Wherever he went the people obeyed his words, sinners were reconciled, vocations became numerous, and the ardor of the apostolic life burned with all its original brightness.

In the month of September 1226, Anthony suspended for a time his apostolical labors to assist, with the other superiors in France, at the provincial chapter of Arles. Both old and young eagerly gathered about him and regarded him as the glory of their Order. They congratulated him for the strong blows he had given to the hydra-headed heresy of the Albigenses. But Anthony was not at all flattered by their warm compliments; even as the patriarch of Assisi, his model, he referred everything to God.

Talents and heavenly favors and personal merits recommended the Portuguese wonderworker to the suffrages of his brethren. They elected him custodian of Limoges unanimously, that is to say, superior of two or three convents in the city. But Anthony was equal to the task assigned him.

A fortnight after his election, on the fourth day of October 1226, the patriarch and founder of the Franciscan Order gave up his pure soul to God. Anthony inherited with the mantle of Francis not only a part of his authority, but his virtues, his humility, his mildness, and his zeal.

THE WONDER-WORKER AT LIMOGES

The city of Limoges gave the wonderworker one of those triumphal receptions which explains the faith of that epoch. The people wished to see him, to hear him, to touch the hem of his garments. He had scarcely set foot in the city before he preached in the cemetery of St. Paul. On the following day it was the abbey itself which claimed his presence. The Benedictines of Mount Soubase had respectfully received the seraphic patriarch and had furnished him with his first place of prayer. Their brethren of Limoges surrounded the privileged disciple with the same veneration and extended him equal assistance. His coming to their monastery is mentioned as an event. The guardian, however, did not neglect the direction of the religious confided to his care. He strengthened the good, enkindled ardor in the slothful, and had pity for the wavering. One of this latter class, a novice named Peter, discouraged for the moment, was tempted to return to the world. The saint was warned by a revelation of the temptation and the interior agonies of the novice. St. Anthony went to him and, breathing on him, said, "Receive the spirit of strength and wisdom." The novice at once fell to the ground as if dead, while his soul was ravished by ecstasy and transported among the splendors of heaven. When he recovered his senses he wished to speak of the heavenly wonders his soul had contemplated, but the saint hindered him. The temptation had passed away and the novice became an exemplary religious.

At Limoges his preaching excited an indescribable enthusiasm. It became necessary to preach in the open air, for no church was large enough to contain the multitudes that flocked to hear him.

To true and loyal souls who asked the assistance of his prayers, the wonderworker refused nothing. The following is a striking example: A certain lady of Limoges who was a great benefactress of the Friars was one day severely reproached for it by her husband. In a fit of anger and jealousy he went so far as to tear out her hair. Sorrowfully she sought the wonderworker, related what had happened, and asked him to restore her hair. The request seemed somewhat singular to St. Anthony, and a smile which looked like a refusal played about his lips. But, touched by the tears of the lady, he cast himself on his knees, and while he prayed the hair grew again, as if under the action of an invisible hand. But what was still more remarkable, the husband, struck by this marvel, repented, was reconciled with his wife, and vowed to the Franciscans an affection which lasted his lifetime.

At Limoges the name of St. Anthony was hailed with delight, and this admiration spread to the whole region.

All the cities of Limousin disputed the honor of the wonder-worker's company. He yielded to their requests when he could, taxing his strength without ever considering difficulties, and sowing miracles at every footstep.

At St. Julien he predicted that the improvised pulpit from which he spoke would be overthrown, but, notwithstanding the efforts of Satan, no serious result would follow. The prediction was fulfilled. The staging fell in the tumult at the beginning of his discourse, but no one was injured.

By a spiritual favor St. Anthony recompensed the abbey of Solignac for the generous hospitality the sons of St. Benedict had shown him. A poor monk of the monastery, tempted like St. Paul by the demon of impurity, could find no rest either day or night. He opened his soul to the powerful wonderworker, who clothed him with his tunic. The shadow of St. Peter healed the sick, the robe of St. Anthony was no less efficacious. From this robe, sanctified by contact with a virginal flesh, went out a virtue which appeased the storm of the senses and delivered forever the monk kneeling at his feet.

Again, there was a poor sinner so stifled by emotion and repentance for his faults that he could not speak so as to make his confession. "Go," said the saint, "and write your sins on a sheet of parchment." The penitent obeyed; he returned in about an hour, bringing a sheet wet with tears and containing a long list of his sins. But as fast as he declared them an angel effaced them, and when he reached the end, the page was white and without stain.

Everywhere, in the cities as well as in the country, theinvincible champion of God's rights created extraordinary interest. People from all ranks of society sought him out. All sorrows, whether physical or moral, appealed to him. Everyone blessed him, but especially the lonely, the homeless, the sick, and sinners.

It must be mentioned that mothers were especially anxious, and women in general were most enthusiastic about him. Endowed with religious instinct deeper than that of men, the women eagerly pressed about his pulpit to assist him in his poverty, or to defend him against the calumnies of the Manicheans. In return he consoled them in their sorrows, strengthened their weakness, blessed their children, and lavished on them the most splendid miracles. These were most touching because they referred to what was most sensitive—a mother's sorrow.

It is related that a woman who was preparing **a** bath for her child, on learning that the saint had arrived in the village, hastened to hear and see him. In her haste she placed her little child in a boiler of scalding water instead of in a bath of tepid water. On returning from the sermon, she had a presentiment of her mistake. She ran, more dead than alive, and found her son in the boiling water, it is true, but smiling and without the slightest injury. In another place a lady, on returning from an instruction given by the apostle at Limousin, found her child dead in its cradle. We can imagine the mother's sorrow at a catastrophe so cruel and so unexpected. A thought of hope, however, crossed her mind. Perhaps the powerful wonderworker would restore her child! She returned to him weeping, but confident, and from her broken heart escaped this maternal cry: "My son is dead! Have pity on the tears of a mother!" "Go," answered the saint, in an inspired tone, "the good Lord will have pity on you." She believed his word, returned in haste, and found her son not only alive but in all the vigor and freshness of his young life, amusing himself with his little toys.

It was amid these wonders, and many similar ones, that the apostle went through the neighborhood of Limoges. He scattered graces and heavenly favors, even as the husbandmen sow the seed, with full hands, until the people spoke of him in their picturesque language as the *sower of miracles.*

And when he had finished his mission in one place ne continued his course, walking through the frost and snow barefoot, always unmindful of himself, always in search of the lost sheep. The consoler of souls, he was himself consoled by sight of the good he had done them; not infrequently he mingled with the people and shared their joys and sorrows.

One day he entered the house of a rich and pious man who had offered him the hospitality of his manor. This man hardly suspected the grace which he was about to enjoy. The gentleman assigned him a room separated from the others, so that he might have more freedom in his exercises of piety and contemplation. While the blessed Anthony prayed alone in his chamber the proprietor visited the tenants of the manor. Suddenly his solicitude and his devotion for the saint prompted him to look towards the place where he prayed; through the window he saw in the arms of Anthony a child of great beauty who embraced him with tenderness. The saint, on his part, returned the caresses and kisses; and not for an instant did he take his eyes from the beautiful child. Pale with emotion, and beside himself at the sight and the beauty of the child, the gentleman asked himself whence the charming little one had come. He was not the victim of an illusion; the spectacle which he witnessed was a reality. The blessed Anthony was conversing intimately with Jesus, the Son of God and of the Virgin, who had come from heaven to console His servant. The mere mention of the name of Jesus caused his heart to beat with joy; now he conversed with Him face to face, as with a friend, and with touching familiarity. In his humility he seemed embarrassed by the miracle which had just happened. He could not, however, conceal it from his host, for the Holy Infant Jesus revealed to Anthony what the man had seen. This is why, after the Infant had disappeared, he forbade his host to reveal what he had seen as long as he lived. But after the death of the blessed Anthony the gentleman' divulged the secret of the vision just recorded. He made the deposition solemnly while shedding torrents of tears.

From this time Anthony strove to show the Heart of Jesus as the principle of supernatural life; as the golden altar on which burns night and day the incense which arises in odoriferous clouds towards heaven and embalms the earth. He felt especially an insatiable desire to adore, to thank, and to annihilate himself before God and to remain alone with Him. From Chateauneuf, where he had just enjoyed the vision described, he went to Brive. There he found in the neighborhood of the city a kind of desert where he founded a hermitage like Mount St. Paul. He dug out a grotto in the rock near a fountain of limpid water and abandoned himself to the delights of contemplation. In this solitude he established three or four postulants who had left the world to be near him. After his departure he left them there. Wonders accompanied him even in the desert. His poverty there was extreme; everything was wanting except courage and the love of God. In a moment of distress, the venerated guardian asked a lady of Brive to assist the little community and to send some vegetables. This she did gladly, in spite of a severe and persistent rainstorm, which was enough to paralyze the most energetic good-will; yet she charged her servant to carry the treasures of her charity to the hermitage. On her return the faithful messenger related to her mistress with admiration that she had walked all the way in the heavy rain, and that not a single drop reached her.

This fact reminds us that nothing is small which is done in a spirit of faith, and the good Lord never fails to recompense, whether it be sublime devotion, or the cup of cold water given in His name.

Solitude is the home of strong souls. There the air is pure, peace most profound, and converse with God most easy. It is not astonishing that the angel of darkness, this abiding enemy of the human race, seeks to disturb the echoes, especially when he has before him apostles who take from him his victims. One evening during the prayer which follows the song of compline, the companions of St. Anthony saw a band of thieves occupied in destroying the harvest of a neighboring field which belonged to one of the principal benefactors of the convent. They ran to warn the blessed Anthony. He said to them: "Be not deceived. This is an artifice of the demon, who strives to turn you away from the exercise of the presence of God." Early on the following day the harvest was intact, and the religious were again witness of in what large measure the soul of their superior was adorned by the gifts of the Holy Spirit.

ST. ANTHONY LEAVES FRANCE

No one wept more bitterly for the loss of the seraphic Francis of Assisi than St. Anthony. No one prayed with more fervor, that from the highest heaven he would still watch over his children and place at their head another like himself, a man capable of organizing and guiding an institution so necessary for the welfare of the Church. He was charged by his brethren, with a special and secret mission to the Supreme Pontiff, a mission relating probably to the candidature of Father Elie, from whom was feared innovations and laxities which ought to be avoided. He left Limoges in February 1227, for the banks of the Rhone and journeyed towards Marseilles. This voyage was rapidly accomplished and was signalized by a marvelous act of gratitude.

When he and his companion, covered with sweat and tired out, reached a little town of Provence, a poor woman, touched by compassion, invited them to come and rest at her house. She received them as generously as Martha received Our Lord at Bethany. Impelled by charity, she placed bread and wine on the table, and ran to borrow a glass from her neighbor. But, either through inadvertence or awkwardness, the companion of the saint, in placing the glass on the table, broke it in two pieces. Then another accident still more unfortunate happened; the hostess, in returning to the cellar, saw that she had forgotten to close the spigot of the cask, and the wine had flowed on the ground. This was a severe loss for her. She could not contain her grief and informed her two guests of what had happened. The blessed Anthony, covering his face with both hands that he might pray more easily, implored the Author of all good to have pity on the affliction of such a generous Christian, and not allow her good work to go unrewarded. His prayer ascended like an arrow to the very throne of God. Suddenly the cup and the stand of the glass were united. The poor peasant was astonished at this, but realizing that it was a miracle, and persuaded that he who could perform such a prodigy could also perform another and restore to her the lost wine, she ran to the cellar. There a new surprise awaited her. Her cask of wine was full and running over as if from the winepress. Delirious with joy, and beside herself, she did not know how to express her gratitude. But always humble, detached from everything and from himself, the wonderworker shrunk from the praises and the marks of veneration which he considered should be given only to God.

The prayers of a saint are powerful, and his benedictions a germ of resurrection and of life. The Albigensian heresy, a work of perfidy and valence, was to disappear, even as the darkness disappears before the first rays of the morning sun. Truth must regain its empire, and, in the words of St. Louis, France would attain the fulness of her glory. France, on her part, is not ungrateful to St. Anthony. She gives him a place side by side with St. Dominic in the devotion, the honor, and the admiration she gives to her deliverers, to those chosen men whom

Providence sends her in wicked times to save her from anarchy and error.

Rome, at the time when the blessed Anthony went there, was preparing to celebrate the feasts of Holy Week. These feasts are more imposing there than any place else in the world. The streets are crowded with strangers of every tongue and country. The churches are adorned with their richest decorations. What a source of pure and strengthening emotions it must have been for the son of Theresa Tavera to see Rome, to visit her in the midst of that religious pomp which surpasses everything here on earth; to go through the places sanctified by the presence of the patriarch of Assisi!

Unknown, mingling in the crowd of pilgrims, Anthony was free to satisfy every wish of devotion, and could taste of those legitimate joys which inspire great and holy memories. He could do all this quietly, and yet not without being remarked. Seeing him pray with so much fervor at the tomb of the Apostles, or kiss with respect the arena of the Coliseum—this arena stained by the blood of so many martyrs—the pilgrims asked in astonishment who was this monk of angelic appearance.

The chair of St. Peter was at that time filled by a Pope most favorable to the Franciscans, Gregory IX., the friend, the protector, and the counsellor of the patriarch of Assisi. He was not content with merely receiving the homage and the petitions of the privileged disciple of St. Francis; he went farther. Learning by public rumor of the virtues and the merits of the wonderworker from Portugal, he selected him to announce to the people the indulgences of the Holy Week, and to preach the crusade against the infidels. The order came from a. source too high for the blessed Anthony to answer otherwise than by a filial submission.

This was done to stir up the masses. And he certainly did stir them by the magic of his words and by his sanctity. He led them in the bitter pathways of penance and instituted at Rome the Confraternity of the Flagellants—a confraternity which had for its object to honor the mysteries of the Passion and to expiate the iniquities of men.

The day of Easter witnessed the renewal of the miracle of Pentecost. An innumerable multitude eagerly pressed about the saint's pulpit. Greeks and Latins, Slavs, French, English, and Germans, all heard him distinctly speaking, each in his own tongue.

St. Anthony made giant strides in the way of the apostolate. Nothing could arrest him, neither the acclamations of the pilgrims nor the wonders of art. Fortified by the blessing of Gregory IX., he left the eternal city on the day following the paschal feast and turned his steps to Assisi.

When he beheld this little city, the home of St. Francis, suspended like an eagle's nest on the side of Mount Soubase, his heart beat violently. At length he could at leisure satisfy his filial devotion for him whom he invoked as a saint. To visit the Portiuncula, the cradle of the Order, Our Lady of Angels, the scene of the apparitions of the Virgin Mother, the cell which had received the last sigh of the seraphic patriarch, was one of the sweetest joys of his life. He went to the ancient city and entered the church of St. George, where the mortal remains of the founder rested temporarily. Anthony closely pressed his lips to the stone of the tomb, and there prayed for a long time. His prayers and his sacrifices had no small bearing on the result of the Chapter General of Assisi, which chose John Parent of Florence, a man of eminent mind, of frank and loyal character, as the immediate successor of St. Francis. Anthony was named provincial of Bologna.

ST. ANTHONY IN ITALY—THE MIRACLE OF THE FISHES

As soon as Anthony had regulated the affairs of his province, he took up the cross and hastened to the people who had been captured by heresy in Italy, as well as in France and Germany. They were the Cathares, or Patarins, who were very numerous in Roumania and in Emilia; the Circoncis in Lombardy; the Vaudois, entrenched in the Milanese and in the mountains of Piedmont. These sects were only varieties of the same heresy with which the Albigenses connected themselves, and they made great inroads in the south of France.

Faithful to his old methods, Anthony commenced by protecting the poor people against the seductions of the Manichean heresies. The lowly were dear to him. To him they were the cherished lambs of the flock of Christ. He led them to the pastures of the true faith. He quenched their thirst at the pure and sacred sources which flowed from the opened side of the Savior. But, like the good shepherd, he did not take flight at the coming of the wolves who raged about the flock. He went out to meet them and endeavored to subdue them.

Rimini had become the camp of the Cathares. A man less resolute than Anthony would have hesitated to enter this discontented and rebellious city. He, however, enters it, having decided to announce the word of truth, in season and out of season, to convict the shameless sectarians of error and perfidy, and to threaten them with the judgments of God. But his eloquence, usually so attractive, from his frank and courageous manner, produced no effect. The Cathares, angered at the zeal with which he attacked them, would not yield, even so far as listening to him. They remained harder than stones; not content with refusing to give ear to his reasoning, they left him to preach by himself.

But Anthony was not discouraged. He turned his eyes towards heaven. In prayer he shed abundant tears until the inspiration of grace came to his aid. He conceived the idea of preaching to the sea, since the earth responded so badly to the appeals of his charity. By bringing man to a school of dumb irrational creatures, he wished to give him a solemn lesson. He hoped to take away from the Cathares all their influence over the people since they would not yield to manifest truth. God sustained the faith of His apostle.

St. Anthony then went to the shore where the river flows into the sea. Standing there, between the river and the sea, he cried out in a loud voice: "Hear me, ye fishes of the sea. It is to you that I am about to announce the Word of God, since the heretics refuse to listen to it."

At the sound of his voice the waters trembled; the countless tribes which inhabit them hastened to range themselves as if in battle array, the smallest in front, the largest in the rear, with every head turned towards him who had called them. "My brethren," said the wonderworker to them, "you owe your Creator a boundless gratitude. He it is who has assigned to you as a dwelling this noble element and these immense reservoirs. He it is who provides for your refuge in tempests the depths of the waters, gives you fins to go whither you will, and furnishes you with your daily food. In creating you He has commanded you to increase and multiply and blessed you. At the universal deluge, while other animals perished in the floods, He preserved you. He honored you by selecting you to save the prophet Jonas, to furnish tribute to the Incarnate Word, and to serve Him as nourishment before, as well as after, His resurrection. Then praise and bless the Lord who has favored you among all created beings."

Attentive, as if they had been endowed with reason, the fishes testified by their movements to the pleasure they took in listening to the saint, and that they wished to render to the Most High the mute tribute of their homage. "See," said the apostle, turning to the multitudes, "see for yourselves how creatures devoid of reason hear the Word with more docility than men created to God's likeness."

When the news of this wonder was reported all the inhabitants of the city hastened to Anthony. The Cathares themselves yielded to the popular enthusiasm and were witnesses of the dominion which the apostle exercised over the sea. The spectacle touched them and falling at the feet of the wonder-worker, they begged of him to instruct and enlighten them.

Thus, they came of their own accord, anticipating his own desires. At last, the faithful rejoiced; the heretics opened their eyes to the splendors of the faith. During this time the fishes listened and applauded in their own way without departing. They seemed as if awaiting the blessing of the saint before resuming the liberty of their sports. He blessed them, dismissed them, and at once they dispersed in every direction, according to the instincts which guide them in the waters.

The wonderworker remained several weeks at Rimini to reap the fruits of his victory. They were most abundant. One of the principal leaders of the sect named Bouvilla, bound for thirty years in the bonds of heresy, publicly retracted his errors. His abjuration was most remarkable, and he was followed by most of his co-religionists.

Some of them, however, furious at their defeat, resolved to be avenged by poisoning their adversary. They invited the apostle to dinner and gave him poisoned meat to eat. The saint, who knew by revelation of the infernal plot which they had planned against his life, reproached them. They were not in the least disconcerted, and adding irony to their cruelty, they endeavored to ensnare him by a dilemma from which he could not escape, so they thought, without admitting he was conquered. "Either you believe in the Gospel or you do not. If you believe in it, why do you doubt the accomplishment of the prophecy of your Master who promised that His disciples should cast out demons, and poisons should not injure them? If you do not believe in the truth of the Gospel, why do you preach it? Take this poison and if it does not injure you, we swear to you to embrace the Catholic faith." "I will do it," replied the intrepid missionary; "not to tempt God, but to prove to you how much I have at heart the salvation of your souls and the triumph of the Gospel." Then making the sign of the cross on the poisoned meats, he ate them without experiencing the least inconvenience; and the angels inscribed in the golden book of the elect a new victory and new names. The heretics kept their word, and, sincere and convinced, re-entered the fold of the Catholic Church.

The wonderworker had entered Rimini saddened and in tears; he left it amid popular ovations. All the people accompanied him to the port, where he embarked for Illyria, and the reconciled Cathares were not the least enthusiastic in their acclamations. He traversed the Adriatic, landing on the shores of Illyria, and evangelized all the seashore of the gulf of Trieste, from Aquilla to Venice, passing by Goritz, Udine, Gemona, and Conegliano. Here he attacked the Patarins in their last entrenchments; there he restored to the degenerate Christians the integral faith of their baptism.

The blessed Anthony was at Gemona, near Udine. He had accepted a foundation in that city, and he himself superintended the work of construction. Seeing a peasant passing near the lumberyard in a cart drawn by two oxen, he asked him to lend his cart to carry some bricks and lumber. The peasant answered it was "impossible." He was not inclined to give gratuitous service. "I am carrying a dead man," he said. He told a falsehood, for the pretended dead man was his own son who was lying asleep in the cart. Shortly after the peasant endeavored to awaken his son to tell him how he had fooled the monk-mason. But he tried in vain. He had spoken the truth without knowing it, when he said he carried a dead man. At the sight of the corpse he was seized with fear and repentance. He left his cart and oxen and ran to cast himself at the feet of the wonderworker, conjuring him to pardon his falsehood and restore him his son. The sorrow of a father is something sacred. The saint returned with the peasant to the funeral cart, made the sign of the cross on the corpse, and gave his hand to the young man now restored to life and health. To do good to those who do evil to you is the vengeance of the saints.

On the first of the following year the apostle left Gemona and travelled rapidly through Trevise and Venice, as he was anxious to see his convent and his brethren at Padua.

ST. ANTHONY
AT PADUA

Padua is the scene in which God wished to manifest the most abundant treasures of grace with which He had enriched the soul of His servant. Padua will bear his name in the records of the Order of the Friars Minor. From Padua he receives his name. But Anthony is not thinking of this. On looking out upon the city he thought of the ravages which the heretics had wrought in it. Then his heart was moved with compassion and yearned for the people. He wished to lead back the wandering children and warm them at the fireside of the charity of Jesus Christ.

He arrived at Padua with the reputation of a saint and of an incomparable orator, and at a most opportune moment. As Ash Wednesday was at hand, and the Lenten time was about to open, the bishop of Padua entreated him to preach the Lenten devotions. The apostle yielded to the wish of the prelate and put his hand to the work at once.

This station proved most fruitful in conversions and miracles. Although sick and suffering, Anthony preached every day, and in the ardor of his faith and his charity seemed to gain supernatural strength. The people came to his sermons from all the cities and from villages several miles around. The roads were lined with pilgrims, anxious to hear the eloquent voice whose accents aroused the world. More than thirty thousand persons pressed about the pulpit of the wonderworker; bishops, prelates, religious of all orders, the clergy and nobility of Padua regarded it as an honor to assist at his sermons. They listened in silence and recollection when the holy man arrived. At his approach not a sound, not a breath was heard; every eye was fixed on him with anxious curiosity. His face was beautiful but pale and bore marks of suffering. When he spoke every soul received with happiness the heavenly seed which he scattered and sowed among them, and when he left the pulpit, had not some strong men protected him from the demonstrations of respect and admiration of the multitude, he would have certainly fallen under the weight of their transports of faith and love.

To speak of the results of this last preaching is well-nigh impossible. Heretics were converted, the most hardened sinners led back to the practice of good, prisoners set free, the poor assisted, the sick healed, etc. Such are the new titles which won for Anthony the veneration of men. In the great city of Padua, where the clergy were so numerous, there were not enough priests to hear the confessions of the faithful. Miracles took place every day. One day the saint met a poor man carrying his little daughter who was afflicted with epileptic fits and was deformed in both feet. The sorrowing father approached the saint, and, laying the child at his feet, begged him to make the sign of the cross over her. Touched by the poor man's faith, the saint blessed the sufferer with the sign of the cross, and she was immediately cured. At another time a noble lady, on returning from a sermon, fell into a deep and muddy ditch and arose without accident. She had recommended herself to God, through the merits of the apostle. At another time twenty-two robbers came, in the middle of the sermon, to cast themselves at the feet of the saint, giving every sign of a true conversion and asking pardon for their iniquities. And again, a woman, as virtuous as she was beautiful, who had been slain by her husband in a paroxysm of jealousy, was recalled to life by the saint, who made the sign of the cross over her. One day a lady, who was prevented by her husband from assisting at the sermon, went to her room, and from her window distinctly heard all the words of the preacher, although she was very far distant. Again, while the saint was at Padua, a youth, named Leonardo, accused himself in confession of having, in a fit of passion, kicked his mother so violently as to throw her down. Wishing to make the young man understand the enormity of his offence, St. Anthony said to him: "The foot that kicks father or mother deserves to be cut off." The penitent, who was of a weak mind, understood these words literally, and going home, took a hatchet and chopped off his foot. The news of this unfortunate occurrence soon spread throughout the city, and coming to St. Anthony's ears, he hurried to the youth's home. Making the sign of the cross over the mutilated limb, the saint applied the dismembered foot to the stump, when they immediately joined and healed without leaving a scar.

St. Anthony spread peace about him, even as the rose spreads its perfume. He gave peace to souls that were severely tried. He did not, however, always keep this privilege for himself, since the angel of darkness frequently made fierce and terrible assaults on him. One night, at the beginning of Lent, the demon appeared to him in a visible form, seized him by the throat, and endeavored to strangle him. Anthony at once invoked her who is more terrible than an army in battle array: "O glorious Sovereign!" Hardly had he pronounced these words when the enemy of man took his departure.

The Queen of Heaven visibly blessed the zeal and the efforts of her devoted servant. The Lenten services had been remarkable for wonders of every kind. The feasts of Easter were a worthy crowning for them. Padua celebrated the triumph of Christ. She sang also the triumph of Anthony and the renovation of souls.

GENERAL CHAPTER OF ASSISI

In the course of the summer of the year 1228 the blessed Anthony set out for Bologna, the place of his residence. He stopped at Ferrara, which was on the way. There our hero had not to combat heresy but only to uproot the vices which dishonor faith, and wherever they are found invariably increase the number of fallen humanity. The church of Saint Mary del Vado was his chosen sanctuary and the principal scene of his preachings. He praised, with his heart full of gratitude, the eminent prerogatives of her whose beauty he had seen in his ecstasies. As he advanced in his apostolic career, his devotion to Mary increased and his confidence became more unalterable.

In the meantime, our saint received from the General of the Order, John Parent, the difficult mission of establishing peace in Florence, which was torn by two rival factions. Two powerful families disputed among themselves for supremacy and transformed the city into a vast and often bloody arena, to the great prejudice of justice and liberty.

Anthony obeyed all the instructions of the General. He hastened to Florence, and there preached during the Advent of 1228 and the Lent of the following year, and during this long sojourn exercised all the resources of his zeal to extinguish the fire of civil war.

One day he had accepted an invitation to preach at the obsequies of one of the dignitaries of Florence. He selected as his text the words of the Gospel, "Where thy treasure is, there is thy heart also." All at once he stopped. He had beheld the soul of the departed one in the flames of hell, the just chastisement of his usurious injustices and his exactions. "This rich man is dead," he said, in a voice slow and grave, "and he is buried in hell! Go and open his strong box and you will find his heart there." The relatives and friends were astounded and overwhelmed by the statement. They hastened to the house of the dead man, and discovered, as the saint had said, the still warm heart of the departed lying in the midst of his golden pieces. The scene was at once tragic and sad. The minds of all were opened by the thought of eternity. The rival families put aside their arms, and concluded a peace, which, unfortunately, was only of short duration.

After the Lent of 1229 Anthony visited the convents of his province; he made new foundations and preached from place to place in Lombardy. At Varese and at Brescia the saint created new homes of Franciscan life. At Milan, at Verona, and at Mantua, he applied himself particularly to the conversion of the Vaudois and had the happiness to receive very many abjurations of heresy.

In 1228, less than two years after the death of St. Francis, the Supreme Pontiff, Gregory IX., had made his triumphal entry into Assisi, escorted by cardinals, bishops, mitred abbots, and pilgrims from every country. He had placed on the head of the great monastic reformer the crown of the saints and had ordered Father Elie to construct a basilica worthy of the treasure it was to contain. In the spring of 1230, the basilica was ready, and on the 25th of May it was opened by the pontifical commission and received the sacred bones of the seraphic patriarch, temporarily placed in the church of St. George.

The provincial of Bologna was prevented by his apostolical labors from assisting at the feasts of the canonization. The translation of the relics was in a measure a compensation. He was so happy again to see the brethren, to venerate the relics of the holy founder, to cast himself at the feet of his immediate successor, John Parent, and to tell him how peaceful Florence, the pearl of Tuscany, had become.

The ceremonies of translation took place with great pomp and magnificence and was enriched by all sorts of heavenly favors. St. Anthony joined with the people in thanking the Lord for so many graces, and invoking with greater love his blessed father who was now so magnificently glorified.

After the festival of translation came the General Chapter of Minors, which was held as formerly at the Portiuncula.

St. Anthony asked to be discharged from all offices so that he might give himself exclusively to preaching. John Parent was not disposed to grant the request, although legitimate and presented with so much humility; he, however, allowed the saint to select his place of residence. Anthony selected Padua "because of the faith of the people, the attachment he had for them, and for their devotion to the Friars." The General and the Chapter gave him again the most striking testimony of their confidence. He was delegated with Father Leon to solicit from Gregory IX. an authentic declaration of the testament of St. Francis, and to repair, in the name of the brethren, the outrage done to the majesty of the Apostolic See by the more than irregular acts of Father Elie, who, of his own authority, had set aside the entire program prepared by the Pope for the feasts of the translation of the body of the holy founder.

Gregory IX. did not conceal his pleasure at seeing Anthony. The Holy Pontiff had not forgotten the labors of his visitor, and to all his requests he gave favorable replies. It was said that the Holy Father wished to attach him to the pontifical court, and, perhaps, to place the purple on his shoulders. To decline these honors the Franciscan had only to repeat the words of St. Francis: "Lord, my children call themselves Brothers Minor because they occupy the last rank in the Church. Have a care lest you take them away under pretext of raising them higher." The pontiff did not insist, and the humble monk, left to his liberty, turned his steps to the mountains of Alverne. He visited the mountain which had been a witness of the ecstasies of the seraphic patriarch, and also of his stigmata. He kissed the imprint of his feet and pressed his lips to the rock where the seraph with six fiery wings had appeared to him.

After this pilgrimage Anthony returned to Padua. Using the liberty which had been given him by the General Chapter to go and preach where he wished, he turned towards this little city which was always so dear to his heart. Great was the joy of the people of Padua when they saw him again within their walls, and when they learned his decision to fix his abode with them. They were in ecstasies, as if a victory had been gained over an enemy; they did not, however, imagine, nor could they, the glory and the triumph which Anthony brought to them in the folds of his worn and faded cassock.

DEATH OF ST. ANTHONY

St. Anthony gave himself up to preaching with his usual zeal. The people, always anxious to hear his words, went in crowds to his sermons. He preached every day during Lent, and his sermons called forth the same admiration as they did during his first mission in 1228. It may be said that the public enthusiasm increased as the holy man's strength grew weaker. The charity which burned within him made him indefatigable. He preached, instructed, exhorted, he heard the confessions of penitents, and very often remained fasting until sundown. But God sustained the courage of His servant by multiplying miracles about him, which by their number and grandeur recall those we have already related.

After the Lenten time the blessed Anthony went through the countries around Padua, preaching in the villages and hamlets which he met on his way and prolonging the holy exercises of his mission until Pentecost.

In spite of the purity of intention which he brought to all work of the apostolate; he was worn out by his constant occupations in secular matters. This is why he thought of leaving the city and of retiring into solitude, to indulge with greater liberty his inclination for prayer and the study of Holy Scripture. He wrote a letter to his provincial asking permission to follow his wish in this matter. When he had sealed the letter, he left it on his table and went in search of a messenger who would carry it to its destination. When the messenger was found the servant of God returned to his cell to get his letter, but it had disappeared. Then he thought he had acted contrary to the will of God and thought no more of it. Some days afterwards he was much astonished at receiving from the provincial a favorable reply to the request he had made. It is reasonable to believe that an angel, under the appearance of a messenger, had carried the letter to the provincial, to satisfy the pious desires of Anthony, and to prove by a miracle that his request was agreeable to God.

For a long time, the servant of God had known the moment of his death, and now it was at hand; but he did not reveal it to his brethren lest he should sadden them.

About a fortnight before that event, seated on **a** neighboring hillside, he looked over the plain, adorned at this season with all the charms of springtime. He cast his eyes over Padua, which was in fullest bloom, and seemed, as it were, seated in the center of a bouquet of flowers. Then he experienced an interior joy. He rejoiced at the beauty of the situation and at the crown which God had placed on his brow. Turning towards his companion, he prophesied the future glory of the city. He did not say what this glory would be; still less from whom it would come. Subsequent events have cleared up the mystery.

Campo San Pietro, or Campietro, a small village, situated three leagues from Padua, where he found a hermitage under the protection of St. John the Baptist, was the retreat in which the great saint resolved to pass the last days of his life. He was received there at the beginning of June 1231, by a pious gentleman named Tiso, the lord of Campietro, with the respect which would be given an angel and an envoy from heaven. Thanks to the care of Tiso, three cells were built from the trunks and branches of large walnut trees, one for Anthony, the others for his two companions, Brother Luke and Brother Roger. This was the last earthly dwelling of the wonderworker. Shut up day and night in his narrow wooden cell, he filled his heart and mind with heavenly contemplation. Not a sound was heard around or about the place, but everywhere eternal peace and quiet, although numerous pilgrims still came to ask both prayers and advice of the saint. The lord of Campietro sometimes obtained a few moments' conversation with him, and he had the distinguished happiness to receive, at the hands of the saint, the habit of the Third Order.

On the thirteenth day of June, about mid-day, at the time when the saint took his repast with his brethren, he sank down and felt himself fainting away. His companions lifted him in their arms and laid him on a bed of branches. But, warned by this signal that his last hour had come, he expressed the wish to be carried to Padua, to the monastery of the Minors, there to die, assisted and surrounded by his brethren. They took him there on a cart, but so great was his exhaustion that when they reached the gates of the city in front of the Arcella, the monastery of the Clares, his companions advised him to go no farther, but to stay in this place where he could more easily find calm and rest. The sick man consented and entered the hospital where three or four Franciscans resided, almoners and spiritual guides for the daughters of St. Clare.

As soon as he had regained a little strength he confessed with profound sentiments of humility and received absolution. Then filled with a joy for which those who stood near him could give no reason, he intoned in a clear and harmonious voice his favorite hymn, "O gloriosa Demina! Hail, O glorious Sovereign!" His eyes remained fixed on an invisible object which captivated all his attention. "What do you see?" asked his astonished companions. "I see my God," he answered.

Then the brothers wished to have administered to him the Sacrament of Extreme Unction which takes away the last stains from the soul—we must be so pure to appear before God. The saint answered: "I have this Unction within me; it is not necessary, but it is good, however, to receive it." After he had received the Holy Viaticum, he received the Holy Unction with the liveliest faith and the greatest marks of compunction, reciting with his brethren alternately the penitential psalms. He was then silent for about half an hour, when suddenly, in the midst of the sobs of his assistants, he yielded his soul into the hands of God, and slept his eternal sleep. This was on the 13th of June 1231, on Friday, just a little before sundown. Anthony was then thirty-six years old.

The Friars Minor resolved to keep the death of the holy apostle a secret as long as possible. They feared the crowds of people would be too great, and the tumult which might follow. But the sad news quickly spread, and in less than an hour the whole city of Padua knew it. Little children, without having been informed by any one, gathered in groups, and ran through the streets of the city crying, "The saintly father is dead; the saintly preacher is dead. St. Anthony is dead!" This news, proclaimed by the mouths of innocent children, filled the inhabitants of the city with grief. The storekeepers abandoned their shops, and the workmen left their labors; some ran in the middle of the streets inquiring where the saint had died. A vague rumor designated the convent of Arcella as the place where the mortal remains were lying. At once men, women, and children hastened there. Some young men bearing arms from the quarter called the Tete du Pont had already reached there to guard the body and to prevent all disturbance. There was a frightful tumult. In the midst of sobs and tears the people pressed about and jostled each other to see once more him who had been the spiritual father of Padua.

Several religious houses at once disputed for possession of his precious relics. The Clares asked permission to preserve them in their convent. The religious of St. Mary claimed the body as their property; especially, they said, as St. Anthony, in dying, expressed a wish to be buried in the convent of St. Mary. But after many difficulties which seemed insurmountable, it was decided that the body of the venerated father should be transported to St. Mary's convent.

An immense procession started from the episcopal palace to visit the precious relics. At the head of the procession walked the bishop of Padua, accompanied by all the secular clergy and all the religious orders of the city and its environs. Then came the governor of Padua, the nobility and the magistrates and the delegates of the common people, followed by the multitudes. When the usual ceremonies were ended by the prelate, the procession returned to Padua, the dignitaries and the magistrates carrying the body on their shoulders. The funeral cortege passed through the outskirts, as well as through the principal streets of the city. At length they arrived at the church of St. Mary Maggiore, which had become the church of the saint.

This was a grand festival for the people and the city; the houses were draped in white cloth, and the way of the procession strewn with flowers. At each step some splendid miracle took place, and, according to the words of the Gospel, "the blind see, the lame walk, and the dumb speak." The church could not contain the multitudes. The people, for the most part, were compelled to remain outside the doors. The bishop officiated, pronounced the absolution, and sealed the tomb in which the relics of the saint rested.

The tomb of the Portuguese apostle was hardly sealed before it became a center of pilgrimage— the scene of multiplied

wonders—and the bishop solicited the Holy See at once for the honors
of canonization. It was no small consolation for Gregory IX. to hear
the recital of the heroic virtues and the splendid prodigies which
recalled all the wonders of the primitive Church. The Pope ordered
that the judicial information should begin without delay. In about six
months the inquiry was ended, and by an exception perhaps unique
in the history of the Church, less than one year after the death of
the servant of God, in the midst of the pentecostal feasts, on the
30th of May 1232, the infallible teacher, then at. Spoleto, solemnly
promulgated the decree of canonization. At length the pontiff intoned
the *Te Deum,* then the antiphon, *O Doctor optime,* thus publicly
saluting the eminent doctor, the defender of the divinity of the
Incarnate Word, the defender of the Real Presence, the apostle of
Mary's prerogatives, and the wonderworker and saint.

And now a new wonder occurred. The feasts of Spoleto were then
being celebrated, and a spirit of irresistible joy ran through the whole
city of Lisbon. All the bells in the towers, moved by no visible hand,
rang out their joyous chimes, and the inhabitants manifested a joy
for which they could give no reason. It was not until two months
afterwards that they got a clew to the mystery. By a coincidence, in
which the finger of God is visible, the bells of Lisbon, the native city
of St. Anthony, were rung at the same time as those of Spoleto, to
congratulate the Portuguese wonderworker.

On the 13th of June 1232, Padua was ready to celebrate the feasts
of canonization. It was just one year to a day after the death of the
wonderworker. The festivities were splendid beyond all description.
The people were overjoyed. They were children praising their father;
they were captives returning thanks to their liberator.

Along the streets could be seen tapestries and hangings, branches
and flowers strewn in profusion, and joy and gladness were on every

side. The people stopped and congratulated one another. This was not merely enthusiasm, but a kind of delirium prompted by gratitude and by a love which could not be satisfied.

And the same feasts and the same splendors were to be witnessed in Lisbon. Was not Anthony the saint of Lisbon before he became the saint of Padua? By a rare privilege in the life of saints both parents of Anthony assisted at this triumph. O happy mother who could count her son among her protectors in heaven and behold all the people render him such honor! O happy family, so visibly blest by God!

The reader will remember how displeased the Canons of St. Augustine were at the departure of Anthony from their convent, and they did not hesitate to manifest their displeasure openly. But Anthony said on leaving them, "When you hear that I have become a saint you will bless God." These words were a prophecy. As soon as he was placed on the altars, the storm of discord suddenly became calm, and the Canons rivalled the Franciscans in their zeal in proclaiming the praises of their former colleague. From this time a sacred bond existed between them which has never been broken. A bond of eternal and reciprocal friendship now unites the two great religious families, and the union has continued for six successive centuries. Each year, on the 13th day of June, a Canon of the Holy Cross from Coimbra goes to St. Anthony of Olivares, where he pronounces the panegyric of the saint, and presides at all the exercises of the convent. He does this to remind all that from Holy Cross came one of the most beautiful minds of the Middle Ages, and one of the lights of the seraphic Order.

In 1263, thirty-two years after the death of the saint, it was voided to remove his mortal remains from the shrine in the church of St. Mary Maggiore to the high altar of a new church built in his honor by the Friars Minor. Their minister-general, St. Bonaventure, was present at the translation of the body, and on opening the coffin it was found that while the body had crumbled into dust, the tongue, which had sung the praises of the Most High and been the means of converting so many, was incorrupt and of its natural color. Moved by the sight of this miracle, St. Bonaventure exclaimed: "O blessed tongue, which always didst bless the Lord and caused others also to bless Him, now is it evident how highly thou wert esteemed by God!"

THE BREAD OF ST. ANTHONY

In France devotion to St. Anthony has spread with a magnificence equal to that in Portugal and Italy. Todaydevotion to the good saint is livelier than ever. Who is there in France, in. America, or in Canada that does not know the good St. Anthony of Padua? How many circumstances might be related of the vigilance and the power of him who is invoked with such great faith, especially when there is question of finding some lost object? But the power of the wonderworker is not limited to this. How many spiritual and temporal graces have been obtained by the invocation of this amiable saint? And what shall we say of the work called the "Bread of St. Anthony"? This work commenced in a modest oratory of Toulon in France, and in a short time spread throughout all France and then to America and elsewhere.

A young girl of Toulon, named Louise Bouffier, thought of consecrating herself to God under the garb of the Carmelites. She was obliged to put the thought away, however, as she was the sole support of her parents; still she consoled herself by employing all her leisure moments in the work of the foreign missions. A favor obtained through the intercession of St. Anthony awakened in her heart a profound sentiment of gratitude. The statue of the wonderworker was on that very day placed in the corner of the workshop where she was engaged, and thenceforth the good saint looked down upon the labors of the young girl. This was the origin of the countless graces and wonders which awakened public attention. She who had hoped to be a daughter of St. Theresa thus became the propagatrix of the devotion to St. Anthony. But we shall let the girl herself tell of the beginning and the rapid progress of this opportune and consoling devotion. She wrote to Rev. Father Marie Antoine, a Franciscan, and propagator of the devotion to the saint, whose name he bore, the following:

"My Reverend Father:

"You wish to know how the devotion to St. Anthony of Padua began in our city of Toulon.

Like all the works of our good God, it developed quietly and in obscurity. About four years ago, I knew nothing of the devotion to St. Anthony of Padua and had only heard it vaguely asserted that he was the patron of those who wished to recover whatever had been lost.

"One morning, I could not open my store door as the secret lock was found to be broken. I engaged a locksmith, who brought a large bunch of keys, and worked on it for about an hour. Having lost all patience, he said to me: 'I must go for some other tools to force the door; it is impossible to open it otherwise.'

"During his absence, inspired by the good God, I said to myself: 'If you promise some bread to St. Anthony for the poor, perhaps he would open the door without breaking it.' At that moment the workman came, bringing a companion with him. I said to them: 'Gentlemen, allow me, if you please. I have just promised some bread to St. Anthony of Padua for his poor; instead of forcing the door, try once more to open it; perhaps the saint will come to our assistance.' They agreed; and when the first key was introduced into the broken lock, it opened without the least difficulty, as if it were the very key of the door. It is useless to attempt to picture the wonder of all present. From that day, all my pious friends pray with me to the good saint, and the smallest of our sorrows is communicated to St. Anthony with the promise of bread for his poor.

"We cannot but marvel at the graces he obtains for us. One of my intimate friends who witnessed these wonders at once promised a kilogram of bread every day of her life if he would obtain for a member of her family the correction of a certain failing over which she had grieved for twenty-three years. The favor was soon granted, and the failing has never returned. In gratitude she purchased a little statue of St. Anthony of Padua, which she has given me, and we have placed it in a little room so dark that a lamp is necessary to make it visible. This is my back room. Well, would you believe it, Father, every day this little dark room is filled with people who come to pray with greatest fervor. Not only do they pray, but you would think that each one is paid to make known and spread this devotion.

"At one time a soldier, an officer, or captain of a ship about to start on a long voyage comes to promise to St. Anthony one dollar a month for bread, if he reaches his destination safely. Again, a mother asks for her child's health or the success of his examinations. Now, a family asks for the conversion of a dear soul near to death who will not receive the sacraments: then, a servant needs a situation, or a workman seeks occupation,—and all these requests are accompanied by a promise of bread if they are answered.

"Some time ago, I was sent for by an aged lady who was in great suffering. 'Mademoiselle,' she said to me, 'for two years I have prayed fervently to the great St. Anthony to relieve me from the misery in which I live, helpless from rheumatism, not able to remain alone, and not having means enough to keep a servant. I have only a small annuity and many necessities. Each day I have conjured the saint to remove my obligations, and have promised him, in thanksgiving, forty dollars for his poor. He has heard my petition, not according to my wishes, but very much beyond my expectations. I have just inherited nine thousand dollars most unexpectedly. This is why I have sent for you.' As she spoke, tears were in her eyes. Her heart overflowed with gratitude, her hand was generous, and our orphans are happy.

"A certain gentleman in the neighborhood of Toulon owned a place worth at least seven thousand dollars which he wished to sell. He made the greatest efforts to find a purchaser, but no one seemed to want the property. Someone told him of my little oratory. He came there, and while kneeling at the feet of St. Anthony, promised fifty francs for bread. Three days after, the property was sold, and on conditions as advantageous as they were unexpected.

"Towards the end of the bathing season, one of my lady friends, who was a very skillful swimmer, while in the water lost a gold ring set with brilliants. Her sorrow was very great when she realized her loss. The bathers, always numerous on our seashore, hearing of the mishap plunged into the water in search of the precious jewel. One after another they plunged into the depths of the Mediterranean, but returned unsuccessful. The lady on entering her house remembered the power of St. Anthony and made him a promise of bread. Early on the following day she returned to the beach, accompanied by a young man, who at the first plunge found and brought back the prized ring. As the lady is well known in the city, the event produced a great impression.

"St. Anthony blesses those who keep their promises but allow me to say that he rigorously punishes those who neglect their obligations. Here is an example. A lady of Toulon had promised one hundred kilograms of bread to obtain a special favor for one dearly loved. The favor was granted, and she hastened to tell us with great demonstrations of joy. But the debt of gratitude was not discharged. Two months passed. We feared some punishment would follow. Very soon we learned that the dearly loved one had died, and almost suddenly.

"A book would not suffice to contain the miracles which are daily witnessed here through the intercession of our saintly wonderworker."

That little box placed at the feet of St. Anthony, in Mademoiselle Bouffier's rear workroom, if it were possible, could recount many a secret and the reason for many anonymous offerings.

In the beginning, the weekly receipts were from fifteen to thirty francs. In Lafayette Street, it is recalled that the receipts for one day reached the unusual sum of one hundred francs. It is scarcely credible, but now, when the box does not yield more than three hundred francs, it is considered a very small amount. The total amount for the year 1894 was 108,506 francs.

Nothing, perhaps, is so calculated to touch or move the witnesses of these wonders as a visit to this modest box, which, although emptied every evening, is filled again the next day by offerings, the secret of which God alone knows. On seeing the marvelous contents of that inexhaustible box spread out, everyone exclaims, "Are not these several days' receipts?" No, that is the amount deposited in one day.

Oftentimes there are four or five hundred francs in banknotes, in gold pieces, in crowns, or in copper coins, and all these gifts are anonymous. By whom this piece of gold has been deposited, or these small coins, or the banknote for one hundred francs, none but God knows.

"But that which especially causes our joy," wrote Mademoiselle Bouffier to some friends, "is the humility which envelops this dear little work, and, as you know, is the true character of God's work. It is the humility with which each one places his or her offering in the box, without caring if I know them or not. And when evening comes, on opening St. Anthony's box to register the receipts, I find the penny of the poor mingled with the banknotes or gold pieces of the rich. The bread kneaded by the charity of each one bears only one name and can bear no other, the name my dear orphans give it,—'the bread of St. Anthony.'"

It is not a rare thing to find some jewels among pieces of money. We can easily believe that these golden rings represent perhaps aseverer sacrifice, for those who part with them to pay a sacred debt, then the gift of a piece of money. But whether in banknotes or coppers, all the offerings are made with the same generosity and simplicity; and there is no more ceremony in depositing one thousand francs than in depositing a single penny.

But all have promised bread for the poor, they have prayed, and their prayers have been answered. The work has been successful, the difficulty has been overcome, the lost object has been recovered, health has been restored, and some long-time prodigal has at last returned to his father's house. Thanks to St. Anthony!

WHAT IS ASKED OF ST. ANTHONY

Everything is asked from St. Anthony, and there are very few requests
made of him that do not meet with a hearty and generous response.
The joy of the petitioner is frequently manifested in cheerful accents
like this which was sent from Paris: "Unbounded confidence in my
good Saint Anthony of Padua, who knows not how to refuse anything.
I love this great saint with all my heart, and I shall be eternally grateful
to him for all the favors he has given me."

One thing which is often asked of him is the restoration of health.
On the 29th of August, 1894, the following letter was received from
Calvados:

"Mademoiselle:—Saint Anthony has heard our petitions! The
good health we have asked for has been granted, and without the
delicate operation which was greatly feared. In gratitude and in
fulfilment of a promise, we herewith send you thirty francs for bread

for the poor of St. Anthony. We shall send the same amount from time to time, hereafter."

A titled lady of Baroul, near Lille, sent the following on May 18th, 1894:

"I was told of the prodigies wrought by St. Anthony of Padua, and now I cannot sufficiently admire the goodness of this powerful wonderworker. On the 10th inst. I learned that my little niece was attacked by meningitis, and regarded by her physicians as a helpless and hopeless case. At once we began a novena to St. Anthony, with the promise of sending you ten francs for your poor people. Today I am informed she is out of danger. Praise and thanks, therefore, to the good St. Anthony whom no one invokes in vain."

On the 31st of August the pastor of Mount Bernenchon wrote:

"I have the honor of sending you the sum of ninety-eight francs that you may be able to purchase bread for your old people and orphans. This is the votive offering of a parishioner for health obtained through the intercession of St. Anthony of Padua."

September 12th, 1894.

"Mademoiselle:—I am happy to send you herewith the sum of twenty-five francs from the Superioress of our Third Order. She promised this amount if she should preserve her eyesight, which she feared was permanently impaired. Having experienced much assistance, she is most anxious to obtain a complete cure and is satisfied that her eyes will be as perfect as they formerly were."

October 31st, 1894.

"Mademoiselle:—I send you enclosed two banknotes, amounting to one hundred francs, for bread for the poor. The good St. Anthony has obtained for me complete restoration to health. I wish to pay him my just debt."

Paris, November 17th, 1894.

"Mademoiselle:—I thank you for the good prayers you have offered to St. Anthony for the cure of my daughter's eyes. We have been heard; and this good saint has aided us in a manner truly providential. I have promised him a pound of bread every week until my child attains her majority, thus wishing to thank him during many years."

We could not hope to give all the testimonies received in gratitude for favors obtained. Even if we gave extracts, these would make a large volume. We are in receipt of like letters daily. Suffice it to say, that the good St. Anthony has been invoked in every circumstance both spiritual and temporal, and in every instance the favors have been granted and oftentimes more has been obtained than was expected or asked for.

But in conclusion we wish to say a word as to the manner of conducting this work of St. Anthony's bread.

In many churches and chapels there is a statue of the saint; at his feet there is a box destined to receive the requests. To ask a favor from St. Anthony, with the promise of bread for his poor, this is the ordinary way:

The request is written, accompanied by a promise, and it is then placed in the box at the feet of the statue. Any formula may be employed. When the request is granted, the promised offering is placed in the box.

PRAYERS TO ST. ANTHONY

Novena in Honor of St. Anthony of Padua.

It has been asked frequently: "What prayers must be employed to make this novena?" We answer that no particular prayers are prescribed. A prayer, the promise of a gift of bread, a sacrifice, in fact any act of devotion, provided it be sincere. It is recommended to terminate the novena by receiving Holy Communion.

Prayer to Find Lost Things.

O glorious St. Anthony, since God has given thee the power of miracles, a power thou hast exercised for more than six centuries, and since He has given thee in particular the power of finding that which has been lost, I come to thee with the confidence of a child to the best of fathers. Grant me, above all, to find the grace of God, if I have had the misfortune to lose it; grant me to find also my former fervor in the service of God and in the practice of virtue; and as a pledge of these graces, so important for my eternal salvation, grant me to find also the things I have lost. Thus, thou shalt make me experience the presence of thy goodness, and thou wilt increase my confidence and my love for thee. (Our Father.)

Efficacious Prayer to St. Anthony.

Great St. Anthony, I congratulate thee on all the prerogatives with which God has favored thee, beyond all His saints. By thy power death is disarmed, and by thy light error is dissipated; they whom malice strives to crush receive by thy assistance that solace so much desired; the lepers, the sick, and the lame obtain complete health by thy power; storms and tempests are appeased at thy command; the captives' chains are broken by thy authority; through thy care things lost are found; all who invoke thee with confidence are freed from the evils under which they suffer and from the perils which threaten them; in a word, there is no difficulty over which thy power and bounty do not extend. O St. Anthony, powerful intercessor, by all these graces which heaven has given thee I supplicate thee to take paternal care of my soul, my body, of my affairs, and of my whole life, being assured that there is nothing in the world that can injure me, so long as I shall be under the safeguard of such a patron and protector. Present my needs and desires to the Father of mercies, to the God of every consolation, that by thy merits He may deign to strengthen me in His service, console me in afflictions, deliver me from evils, or at least give me strength to bear them for my greater sanctification. I ask these graces for myself and for those who are in the same dangers. O perfect imitator of Jesus, who hast received the special privilege of restoring lost things, I ask of you that I may find which has been lost, if such is the will of God, or at least I ask quiet of mind and peace of conscience, the deprivation of which has afflicted me more sensibly than the loss of everything in the world. To these favors add another, which is to keep me faithful in the possession of the true goods, in a word, that no hostile force can make me lose or separate me from my God, to whom be honor and thanksgiving now and forever. Amen. (Five Our Fathers and Hail Marys.)

Petition to St. Anthony.

Charitable protector of those who have recourse to thee, since thou hast received the gift of miracles, I ask of thee the grace of my conversion and perseverance. Present all my needs before the throne of God, keep from me and from all those who are dear to me sickness, adversity, and disgrace; and by the power of thy prayers obtain for us the best blessings of heaven and earth. Amen.

Prayer to Obtain a Good Death.

Great St. Anthony of Padua, sweet hope of all who implore thee, I prostrate myself humbly at thy feet to obtain by thy powerful intercession the greatest of all blessings, the grace of dying well. Do not allow, I entreat thee, by the pierced Heart of Jesus, that I be suddenly seized by death in the deplorable state of mortal sin; grant that at that last moment I may experience the most profound sorrow for the sins of my whole life, that I may be penetrated with love for Jesus, and full of confidence in the power of His blood which was shed for me; that the last movement of my hands may be to carry the crucifix to my lips, and my last words the holy names of Jesus and Mary; in short that, expiring in the embrace of my sweet Redeemer, I may have the happiness to see Him, to love Him, and to possess Him with thee for all eternity. Obtain this grace also for my parents, my friends, my benefactors and for all who are dear to me, in Our Lord Jesus Christ, to whom be honor and glory with the Father, in the unity of the Holy Spirit forever and ever. Amen.

Litany of St. Anthony.

Lord, have mercy on us.
Christ, have mercy on us.
Lord, have mercy on us.
Christ, hear us.
Christ, graciously hear us.
God the Father of heaven,
God the Son, Redeemer of the world,
God the Holy Ghost, Holy Trinity, one God,
Holy Mary, conceived without sin,

 St. Anthony of Padua, Pray for us
St. Anthony, glory of the Brothers Minor,
St. Anthony, lily of virginity,
St. Anthony, gem of poverty,
St. Anthony, example of obedience,
St. Anthony, mirror of abstinence,
St. Anthony, vessel of purity,
St. Anthony, star of sanctity,
St. Anthony, model of conduct,
St. Anthony, beauty of paradise,
St. Anthony, ark of the testament,
St. Anthony, keeper of the Scriptures,
St. Anthony, teacher of truth,
St. Anthony, preacher of grace,

St. Anthony, exterminator of vices,

St. Anthony, planter of virtues,

St. Anthony, conqueror of heretics,

St. Anthony, terror of the infidels,

St. Anthony, consoler of the afflicted,

St. Anthony, martyr in desire,

St. Anthony, terror of the devils,

St. Anthony, performer of miracles,

St. Anthony, helper of all who invoke thee,

Be merciful, *spare us, O Lord!*

Be merciful, *hear us, O Lord.*

From all evil, Deliver us O Lord

From all sin,

From the snares of the devil,

From pestilence, famine, and war,

From eternal death,

Through the merits of St. Anthony, Through his ardent charity, Through his zealous preaching, Through his desire of martyrdom, Through his strict observance of obedience, poverty, and chastity,

On the day of judgment,

We sinners, *beseech Thee, hear us.*

That Thou vouchsafe to lead us to true penitence,

That Thou vouchsafe to inflame us with divine love,

That Thou vouchsafe to let us ever enjoy the protection of St. Anthony,

That Thou vouchsafe to give us, by the merits of St. Anthony, the gift of true contrition, humility, and contemplation,

That Thou vouchsafe us the grace, through the intercession of St. Anthony, to overcome the world, the flesh, and the devil,

That Thou vouchsafe the assistance of St. Anthony to all who invoke him in their necessities,

That Thou vouchsafe graciously to hear us, Son of God,

Lamb of God, who takest away the sins of the world, *spare us, O Lord.*

Lamb of God, who takest away the sins of the world, *hear us, O Lord.*

Lamb of God, who takest away the sins of the world, *have mercy on us.*

Christ, hear us.

Christ, graciously hear us.

Pray for us, O blessed Anthony.

R. That we may be made worthy of the promises of Christ.

Let us Pray.

Almighty and eternal God, who didst glorify Thy faithful confessor Anthony with the perpetual gift of working miracles, graciously grant that what we confidently seek through his merits we may surely receive through his intercession. Through Christ Our Lord. Amen.

The Responsory to St. Anthony.

Si quaeris miracula,

Mors, error, calamitas,

Daemon, lepra fugiunt,

Aegri surgunt sani.

Cedunt mare, vincula,

Membra resque per-ditas

Petunt et accipiunt

Juvenes et cani.

Pereunt pepcula,

Cessat et necessitas;

Narrent hi, qui sentiunt,

Dicant Paduani.

Cedunt, etc.

Gloria Patri et Filio et Spiritui Sancto.

Cedunt, etc.

W. Ora pro nobis, beate Antoni.

R. Ut digni efficiamur promissionibus Christi.

Oremus.

ECCLESIAM tuam, Deus, beati Antonii confessoris tui
commemoratio votiva laetificet, ut spiritualibus semper muniatur
auxiliis, et gaudiis perfrui mereatur aeternis. Per Christum Dominum
nostrum. Amen.

IF miracles thou fain wouldst see:

Lo, error, death, calamity,

The leprous stain, the demon flies,

From beds of pain the sick arise.

The hungry seas fore-go their prey,

The prisoner's cruel chains give way;

While palsied limbs and chattels lost,

Both young and old recovered boast.

And perils perish; plenty's hoard

Is heaped on hunger's famished board;

Let those relate, who know it well.

Let Padua of her patron tell.

The hungry seas, etc.

Glory be to the Father, etc.

The hungry seas, etc.

V. Pray for us, blessed Anthony.

R. That we may be made worthy of the promises of Christ.

Let us Pray.

O GOD! Let the votive commemoration of blessed Anthony, Thy
confessor, be a source of joy to Thy Church, that she may always be

fortified with spiritual assistance, and may deserve to possess eternal joy. Through Christ Our Lord. Amen.

(An indulgence of one hundred days each time. A plenary indulgence, once a month, if recited everyday.)

O Gloriosa Domina.

Hymn w the Blessed Virgin Mary, that St. Anthony was wont to repeat.

O gloriosa Domina,

Excelsa super sidera,

Qui te creavit provide,

Lactasti sacro ubere.

Quod Eva tristis abstulit

Tu reddis almo germine;

Intrent ut astra flebiles,

Coeli fenestra facta es.

Tu regis alti janua,

Et porta lucis fulgida,

Vitam datam per virginem,

Gentes redempt as, plaudite.

Jesu tibi sit gloria,

Qui natus es de virgine,

Cum Patre et Almo Spiritu.

In sempiterna ssecula.

Amen.

O glorious Virgin, ever blest,
All daughters of mankind above,
Who gavest nurture from thy breast
To God with pure maternal love.
What we have lost through sinful Eve,
The blossom sprung from thee restores,
And granting bliss to souls that grieve,
Unbars the everlasting doors.
O gate through which hath passed the King!
O hall whence light shone through the gloom!
The ransomed nations praise and sing
The Offspring of thy virgin womb!
Praise from mankind and heaven's host,
To Jesus of a virgin sprung,
To Father and to Holy Ghost,
Be equal glory ever sung. Amen.

O Lingua Benedicta.

When St. Bonaventure had the grave opened in which the remains of St. Anthony had reposed for thirty-two years, the tongue of the saint was found well preserved and red as in the days when he preached the word of God.

O lingua benedicta, quae Dominum semper benedixisti, et alios benedicere fecisti: nunc manifesto apparet, quanti meriti exstitisti apud Deum.

V. Ora pro nobis.

R. Ut digni efficiamur promissionibus Christi.

Oremus.

Da qusesumus, omnipotens Deus, qui facis prodigia et mirabilia solus, ut sicut Linguam beati Antonii Confessoris tui post mortem incorruptam servasti, ita nos ejus meritis, et exemplo te semper benedicere et laudare valeamus.

Per Christum Dominum nostrum. Amen.

O blessed tongue! that always blessed the Lord, and made others bless and praise Him; it is now manifest what great merits thou dost possess in the sight of God.

V. Pray for us.

R, That we may be made worthy of the promises of Christ.

Let us Pray,

O ALMIGHTY God, who alone dost perform miracles, grant, we beseech Thee, that, as Thou didst preserve the tongue of Thy holy confessor St. Anthony incorrupt after death, we, through his intercession and after his example, may be worthy of praising and blessing Thee forever.

Through Christ Our Lord. Amen.

St. Anthony's Blessing Against the Assaults of the Powers of Hell.

Ecce crucem Domini! fugite partes adversae; vicit Leo de tribu Juda, radix David. Alleluia!

Behold the cross of the Lord! fly ye powers of darkness; the Lion of the tribe of Juda, the root of David, has conquered. Alleluia!

One hundred days' indulgence once a day.—Leo XIII., May 21, 1892.

Three Prayers to be Said Kneeling Before a Picture of St. Anthony in Affliction or Anxiety of any Kind.

O loving Jesus, source of grace and mercy, I cast myself at Thy feet, and I implore Thee, through the love which St. Anthony bore Thee, and through the compassionate Heart with which in Thy bitter agony Thou didst look down upon Thy Mother from the cross and commend her to the care of St. John, to look upon me, a poor sinner, with the eyes of Thy boundless mercy. Come as my loving Father and God to my assistance in my great need and anxiety. In Thee do I trust, in Thee do I hope. Amen.

(Our Father, Hail Mary.)

O good Jesus, loving Redeemer and Sanctifier! I cast myself at Thy feet, and I implore Thee through the love which St. Anthony bore Thee, and through Thy precious blood shed for us, to turn Thy compassionate and fatherly eyes upon me, a poor sinner whom Thou didst free on the cross from the chains of the enemy. Comfort me in my anxiety and affliction, for in Thee alone do I place all my confidence and my hope. Amen.

(Our Father, Hail Mary.)

O loving Jesus, sure and sole refuge of my needy soul! I cast myself at Thy feet, and I implore Thee through the love which St. Anthony bore Thee, and through Thy love for him which induced Thee to come to him in the form of a little child, and to comfort and caress him, I implore Thee to come to me in my great need and affliction, that I may know how precious is Thy presence in a soul that hopes in Thee.

(Our Father, Hail Mary.)

Prayer.

O truest and most loving patron St. Anthony! **I** implore thee in union with the most loving Heart of Jesus, which He suffered to be opened for sinners after His death, show me how great is thy power before the throne of God, and let me be comforted in my affliction with the hope that, like all who call upon thee in their need, I may **be** able to say with a joyful heart, God truly lives and reigns in His servant St. Anthony. Amen.

Prayer for One who Would Devoutly Honor St. Anthony.

O St. Anthony, my faithful advocate and protector! I rejoice for thy unspeakable happiness in the contemplation of the Most Holy Trinity, in which the soul possesses all that it could ever desire. I earnestly and humbly beg thee to regard not my sins and ingratitude, but, in thy tender compassion, beg Our Lord Jesus Christ to grant me His grace, without which I can do nothing. With this divine gift I shall be strengthened to overcome my evil desires, to discipline the sensibility of my soul, to resist the temptations of the evil one, and amend my bad habits; it will enable me to advance in the love of God, to fulfil the divine will of God as perfectly as possible, to walk in the way of a true Christian life, to recognize and discern between good and evil counsel, to accept with a joyful heart interior as well as exterior admonitions, and to love and serve my neighbor as the divine will decrees.

I also pray thee, O St. Anthony, to protect me against the hands of my enemies, to save me from an .unprovided death; above all, implore God that I may not be surprised by death and depart this life without the sacraments of holy Church, which Our Lord Jesus Christ has instituted to strengthen and comfort us in that dread hour, and that thou and our blessed Mother may be present at my side; and finally that, through the bitter passion of Our Savior and thy intercession, I may, with thee and all the saints and elect of God, rejoice and praise Him forever in the heavenly country.

.